E.D. Nixon

The Unsung Father of the Montgomery Bus Boycott

By
Michael Eaddy

Illustrated by Michael Escoffery

For information on purchasing books, please email:
meaddy200g@gmail.com

Mr. Eaddy can be available for talk-backs, motivational speaking and other live events. For more information, please email:
meaddy200g@gmail.com

Library of Congress Control Number: 2016901016

ISBN 978-0-9972046-0-5 (Hardcover)
ISBN 978-0-9972046-2-9 (Paperback)
ISBN 978-0-9972046-1-2 (eBook)

For Mikkari, my daughter,
you are an extraordinary gift.
Continue to soar.

In loving memory of my godparents:

E.D. Nixon Jr., aka Nick La Tour
&
Alma Johnson.

Your love is everlasting. I kept my promise.

To my dad, I am what I am because of you.

This book is dedicated to E.D. Nixon, who gave his life of service to his people and his community. You are a hero.

Special Thanks

To my wife Sharon,
Carole Terry and Michael Escoffery

I would like to tell you a story about The Unsung Father of the Montgomery Bus Boycott, and the Civil Rights Movement. His name was Edgar Daniel Nixon. Long before Dr. Martin Luther King, E.D. Nixon was the principal black leader in Montgomery, Alabama. He helped spark the Civil Rights Movement. E.D. Nixon was born July 12, 1899 in his family's home on King Street in Montgomery. He was the fifth child of eight. His life was dedicated to the pursuit of social justice.

E.D. Nixon was raised in a religious family. His father Wesley, was a baptist preacher who traveled for long periods of time as an evangelist. His mother Sue Ann, was a maid-cook. The whole family also worked as sharecroppers. Sharecroppers are farmers allowed to use land, in return for a share of the profits, from the sale of the crops. E.D.'s mother died when he was only eight years old. After her death, he and his siblings moved in with his father's sister, Aunt Pinky. Aunt Pinky instilled in him strong moral, and spiritual values. As a child, E.D. loved school. More than anything he wanted to continue his education so he could make a better life for himself. Times were tough back then. Sadly he was forced to quit school. He worked long days in the cotton fields to help support his family. Working in the cotton fields was challenging for young E.D., but he learned the value of hard work.

In the 1890's Jim Crow laws were enacted in the South. These local and state laws enforced racial segregation in public schools, housing, and restaurants. Public transportation was also segregated. After paying their bus fare, blacks, who were also referred to as "coloreds" or "negroes," had to enter through the back door and were only allowed to sit in the back of the bus. They were not allowed to drink from the same water fountains or use the same restrooms that whites used. Racism, poor treatment and violence against people because of their race, was part of daily life. Times were harsh for black people in the South. These unjust Jim Crow laws continued until 1965.

At the age of 25, E.D. was hired to work on the railroads as a sleeping car porter. He greeted passengers, carried bags and shined shoes. He had to be available day and night to wait on them. It also allowed him to meet many train passengers including congressmen, senators, governors, athletes, and other kinds of people. On one trip something happened that changed his life. The train stopped in St. Louis, Missouri. During this stop, E.D. Nixon went to hear A. Philip Randolph speak at the YMCA. He was a well known activist and labor organizer. He became E.D.'s hero. A. Philip Randolph was very influential. He formed the Brotherhood of Sleeping Car Porters, the first all-black union. Just as E.D. had learned the value of work from his Aunt Pinky, he learned organizational skills from his mentor, A. Philip Randolph. This helped Mr. Nixon organize the pullman porters union in Montgomery. Both men fought for better wages, and to advance civil rights for people of color.

On another trip, Eleanor Roosevelt occupied a private car on the train. She was the first lady, the wife of President Franklin D. Roosevelt! E.D. Nixon sought her help in establishing a United Service Organization (USO) military club for colored soldiers. The Tuskegee Airmen and other military servicemen from Montgomery were not allowed in the white's only USO club. Mrs. Roosevelt used her influence to aid E.D. Nixon's efforts. Mr. Nixon found a building downtown on Monroe Street and then Montgomery had its first USO club for colored soldiers.

In 1944, besides his work with the USO, E.D. Nixon also served as the president of the Voter's League. This organization helped increase voter registration. On June 13, of that year, Mr. Nixon led over 750 people on a march to the Montgomery County Courthouse. Their purpose was to register colored voters. Sadly, fewer than 50 people were allowed to register.

The remainder of the people were denied the right to register, due to rules that excluded them. During this decade E.D. also ran for a seat on the County Democratic Executive Committee. This was the first time since Reconstruction that a colored man sought a political office in Montgomery. He nearly won and was only 97 votes short of being elected.

Many people in Montgomery admired and respected E.D. Nixon. They looked to him as a leader. In 1954, E.D. Nixon led a group of 23 students in a march against the segregated William R. Harrison Elementary School. Just like the buses, schools were segregated too.

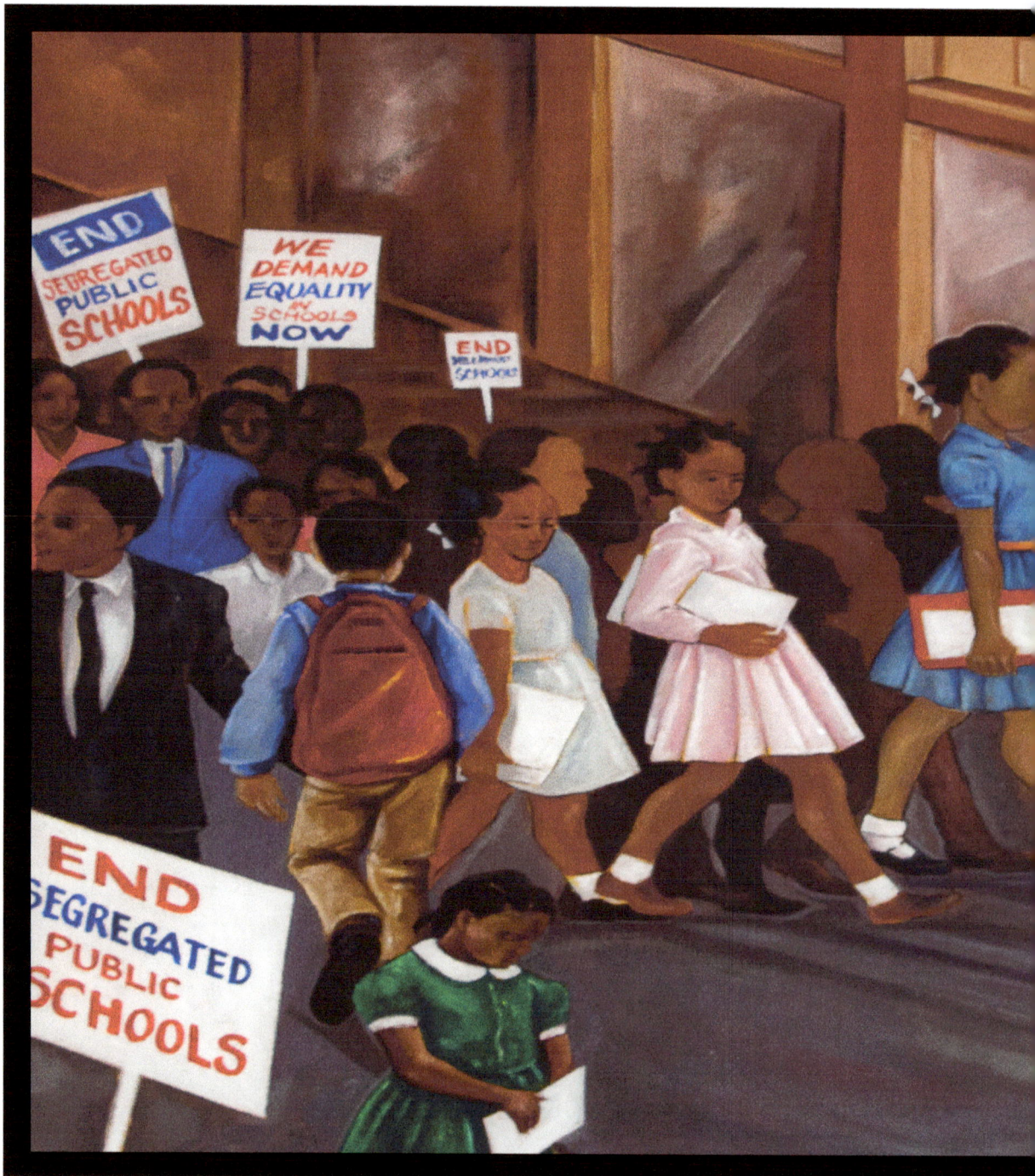

Some colored people in the community were fearful that Mr. Nixon would be targeted for leading marches and for his increasing involvement in civil rights. Even though he was aware of the people's concern for his safety, he always put them before his life. His sense of justice and equality was very strong.

E.D. Nixon was a founding member of the Montgomery Chapter of the National Association for the Advancement of Colored People, commonly known as the NAACP, on both state and local levels. Through the years he remained a dedicated member of this organization, at one time serving as president. E.D. deeply understood the importance of his people winning the right to vote. When voting, an individual has a voice in their government. This is why Mr. Nixon worked tirelessly to register black people to vote. He knew how important it was for colored people to be represented. This was a challenging task because many colored people were afraid to register. They faced threats from whites who wanted to prevent them from registering to vote. These people knew there was power in the ballot! Another method that some white people used to discourage colored people from voting, was to charge them a poll tax as part of the Jim Crow laws. These laws were unfair to some who were poor and who could not afford to pay this tax. Mr. Nixon would often use his own money to pay the poll tax for some people so they could vote.

There was a chill in the air on the morning of December 1, 1955. Rosa Parks readied herself for work at the Montgomery Fair Department Store. After working a long day she was ready to get home to her family. She boarded the bus and took a seat. When a white man boarded the bus, she refused to give him her seat. The bus driver called the police and Mrs. Parks was arrested. Her actions helped chart the course of the Civil Rights Movement. Mrs. Parks was grateful when Mr. Nixon showed up at the jail. E.D. Nixon was with Clifford and Virginia Durr, a white couple who was sympathetic to the cause of negro people.

After Nixon paid the $100 bail, they all went to Mrs. Parks' home. Once there, they discussed plans to break down segregation on buses in Montgomery. Mr. Nixon knew Mrs. Parks had what it would take to challenge the courts. He knew she would make the perfect test case, because she was a real fighter and would not back down.

In the following days, events rapidly began to unfold. After E.D. returned home from the Parks', he began making important phone calls to gather the leaders. His first three calls were to Reverend Abernathy, Reverend Hubbard and Reverend Dr. King. He wanted to persuade these men to support the idea of boycotting the buses in Montgomery. He did, and later that day they met at Dexter Avenue Baptist Church, where Dr. King was the pastor. More than forty leaders were present and they all agreed to a bus boycott. After calling the leaders, E.D. Nixon contacted and met with the city's newspaper editor, Joe Azbell. The boycott was announced on the front page the following day. At the same time, Joanne Robinson and the Women's Political Council were getting the word out by distributing flyers to let the community know about the boycott. Mr. Nixon was asked by Reverend Abernathy to lead the organization, which later became the Montgomery Improvement Association, also known as the MIA. This organization was formed to support the bus boycott. Mr. Nixon declined and suggested Dr. King to be the leader of this organization. Dr. King was elected president, and E.D. Nixon as treasurer at the Mount Zion AME Zion Church. Mr. Nixon recognized King was better suited to lead the Montgomery Bus Boycott. He knew King had a fine mind and strong leadership skills. Most importantly he knew that he was a man of faith who possessed powerful speaking abilities.

As treasurer of the MIA, Mr. Nixon raised over $97,000 to fund the organization and buy station wagons. These cars were used to drive people to and from work so they wouldn't have to ride the buses. This angered some white people who belonged to a racist organization called the Klu Klux Klan, or KKK. A campaign of terror was unleashed on E.D. Nixon. First, they called his home and made death threats. Then they burned a cross on his front lawn. Finally, they bombed his house. Thankfully no one was injured. He was also arrested on made-up charges. Despite all these things E.D. Nixon did not quit. Nixon's leadership, relationship and connection with the community, along with others, helped unite the city.

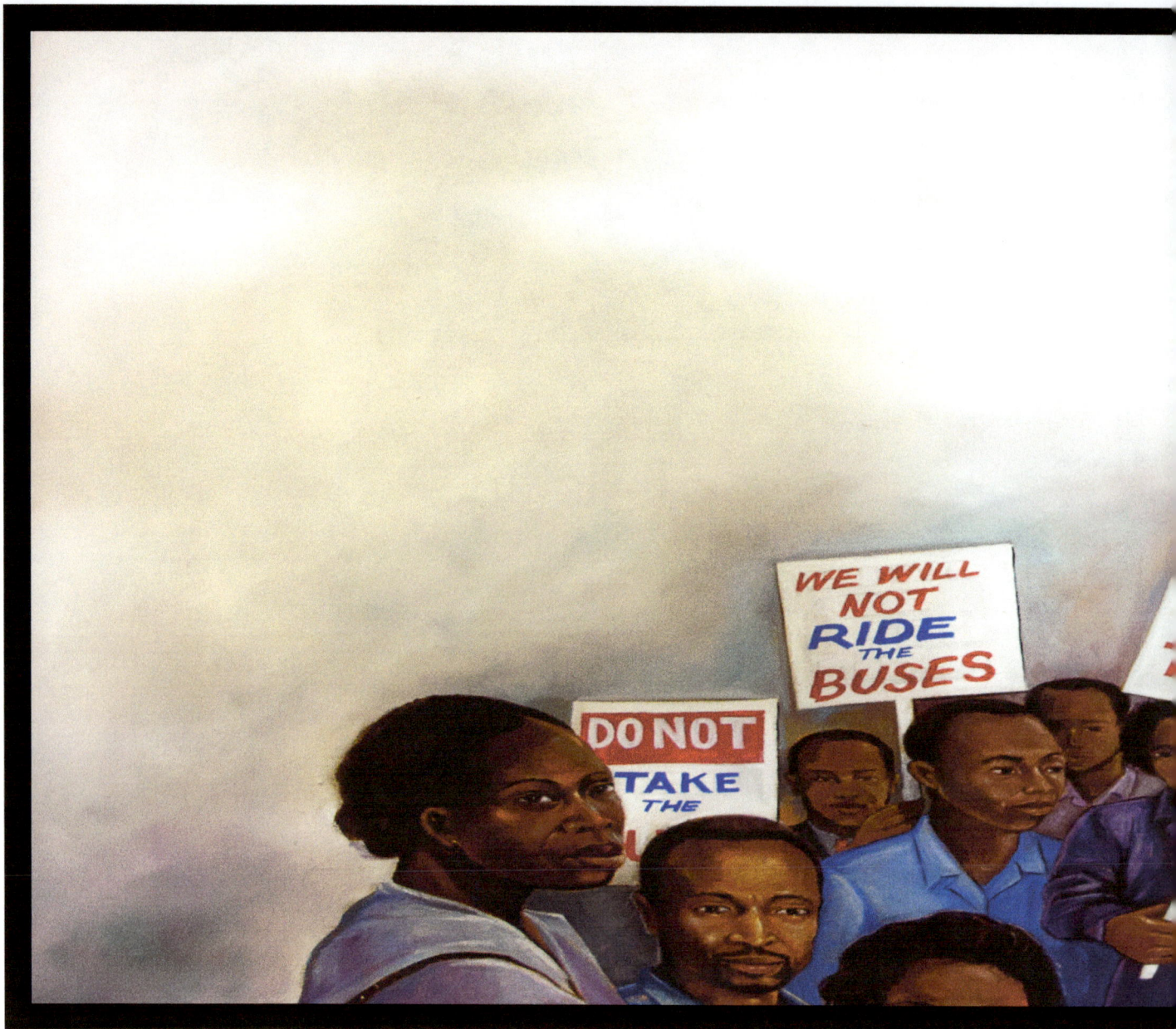

The Montgomery Bus Boycott lasted for 381 days. It was successful in accomplishing its purpose. The bus company lost a lot of money, nearly bankrupting the city's buses. Eventually, a court in Alabama ruled that segregation on the city's buses was unconstitutional. Montgomery's first desegregated bus ride was on December 21, 1956. A feeling of pride and accomplishment, swelled in the hearts of E.D. Nixon, Dr. King, Reverend Abernathy, attorney Fred Gray, and advisor, Glenn Smiley, as they boarded a bus in front of King's home.

Dr. King and Mrs. Parks have received the most notoriety, however, many other people played significant roles in the success of the movement. The most important thing to remember is that the leaders of the boycott and the people of Montgomery were united in their efforts to be treated equally. Their demand for justice was a righteous cause.

E.D. Nixon had little formal education, but it did not keep him from accomplishing great things. He led a life of service to his people and to his community. He was instrumental in advancing the cause of civil rights. He also received four honorary doctorates and met Presidents, Roosevelt and Johnson. On February 25, 1987, E.D. Nixon died at the age of 87. He was truly the unsung father of the Montgomery Bus Boycott.

Michael Eaddy, actor, educator, writer, and motivational speaker, was born in Trenton, NJ. He holds a M.F.A. from Yale University School of Drama, B.F.A. from S.U.N.Y. at Purchase, and a M.S. in Childhood Education from Mercy College, Dobbs Ferry, NY. Michael has appeared in numerous television shows, commercials and theater productions. He is the godson of the late E.D. Nixon Jr. and the late Alma Johnson, E.D. Nixon's niece and advocate. Michael is a Board Director of the E.D. Nixon Foundation, whose mission is to provide mentoring, leadership development and educational opportunities for minority and other under-represented students.

Michael Escoffery, was born in Kingston Jamaica, he has exhibited in over 200 solo exhibitions and over 300 group shows worldwide. He has lived and studied art in California, France, Germany, Hawaii, India, New York , Romania and Turkey, and been the subject of numerous television, radio, newspaper and magazine profiles. His work is published in over 100 books worldwide and in 9 languages. Escoffery's provocative intellect and talent have positioned him at the forefront of the avant-garde as a skilled professional, subjective, and socially conscious artist. Every experience from humor to tragedy, and every object from the sublime to the absured, inspires his imagery. He is outspoken, controversial, and sensitive to his position and responsibilities as an artist.